By Vanessa Wright

Illustrated by Jayda Wentworth

To Miles and Maceo,

You are my inspiration.
Keep praying!

How do we talk to God? We Pray.

Do we speak English, Spanish, or what about Sign Language?

We pray to our Heavenly Father.

He understands all languages.

when we wake up,

we give thanks for a brand new day.

We pray that Daddy doesn't burn our breakfast.

Before we eat,
We thank God for our food.

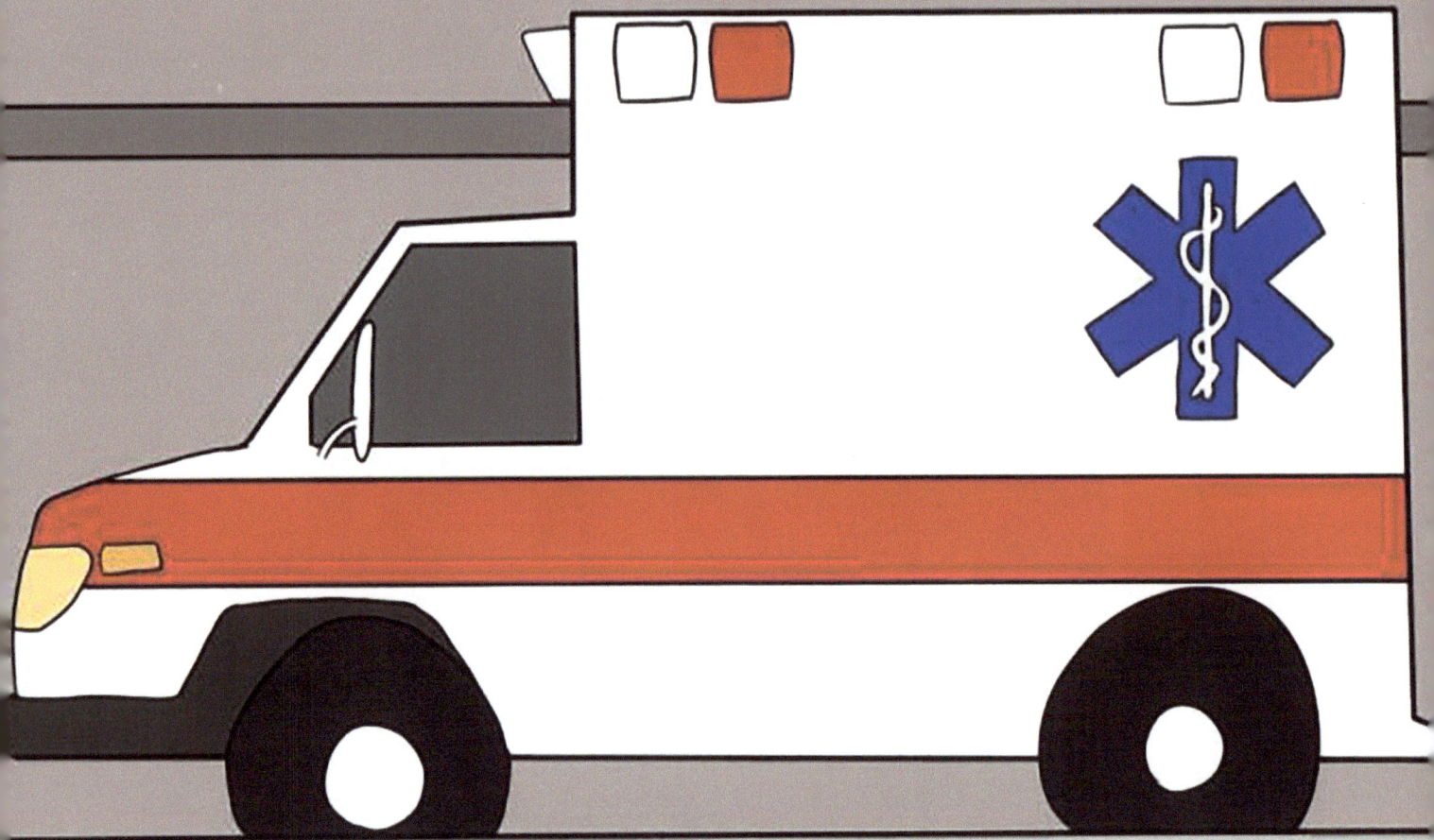

when we see an ambulance,
we ask for healing.

We pray for our neighbors

and friends.

we pray for the homeless on the street.

we pray that Mommy's favorite sports team wins!

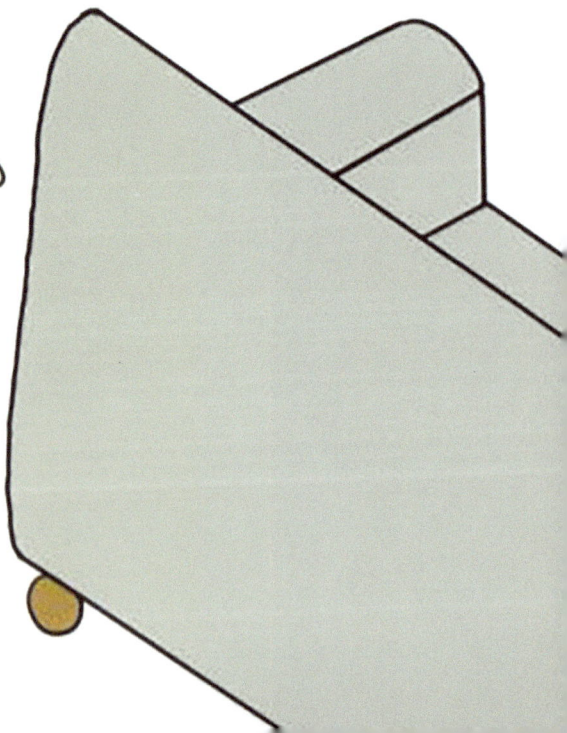

We pray for our favorite superhero.

Before we go to bed, we say:

Dear Heavenly Father, we thank you for this day.

We thank You for our mommy and daddy, grandparents, uncles, aunties, cousins, and pets.

Heal the sick.

Thank You for my brother.
And he thanks You, for me, too!

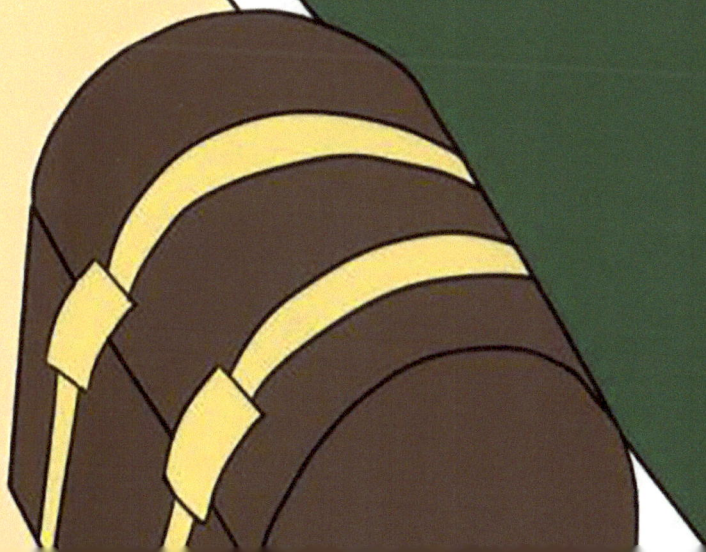

Now, we are ready for bed.

It's time for you to pray; when you are finished, don't forget to say **Amen!**